The Big Picture

Why Network Marketing will boom

EDWARD LUDBROOK

To Vicky

With thanks to Jo Newman and Mike Barker

First published in Great Britain in 1996 by:
Legacy Communications
PO Box 4815
London SW6 4YF

Notice of Liability

ISBN 1-899941-00-2

Cartoons by **Mick Davis**
Designed & Typeset by **Stuart Hammersley**
Printed and bound in Great Britain by **The Schwartz Orginisation**

Foreword

One of the great strengths of direct selling is that it offers a truly universal business opportunity. All around the world, it now represents one of the fastest growing channels of retail distribution. And yet, direct selling has been around for years.

Today, the big difference is how it is organised. Network Marketing is the modern method of distribution made possible by advances in communications and information technology. It's all about supplying goods directly to consumers who like what they have bought, think they are reasonably priced and are happy to pass on personal recommendations.

The rewards come from creating a network of other enthusiastic consumers. You don't have to be a super salesman. To succeed in the business, you just have to like meeting people and be good at organising the efforts of others just like you - most doing the business part-time.

In this excellent little book, Edward Ludbrook puts it all into perspective. He gives some invaluable advice in what to look for in selecting a good business, which is the main task of the Direct Selling Association.

Work with a company with products which appeal to you. Remember that it takes time to build any business. Follow Edward's good advice and I'm confident that you will enjoy your experience.

Good luck!

Richard Berry
Director,
Direct Selling Association

Introduction

In 1989, I attended a meeting and listened to a presentation on a new form of 'low cost franchising' which the organiser claimed to be the Business Opportunity of the 1990's. It was called Network Marketing and it was the most exciting concept I had ever seen or heard.

That night, the presenters claimed many things. They said that Network Marketing was the 'Business of the 1990's, the future of product distribution', and many other things. They were big claims and somehow seemed to make complete sense to me. It was very exciting and I walked out of the meeting three feet in the air.

What amazes me, looking back on that evening and the years that followed, was that I did not ask for any validated facts substantiating these huge claims. I am a person who needs proof. Having come from an economics, military engineering and consulting background, you would think I would want solid evidence that these claims about Network Marketing's future were correct.

In 1992, I became a primary independent advisor to the general public on Network Marketing (sometimes known as Multi Level Marketing). To do my job properly, I had to have a factual, justifiable explanation as to why this industry was going to be a growth industry or I would face the ridicule many others had had to endure. No such explanation was to hand.

After researching this whole subject, I developed my explanation as to why Network Marketing would boom and, since then I have fire-tested this presentation on tens of thousands of people including government officials, business people and financial journalists (who, incidentally, must be the most sceptical people on the planet).

Not one person has ever questioned its accuracy, logic or deductions so I am very confident about its validity. In fact, after listening to my explanation, Business Age, the UK's biggest selling business magazine, conducted its own research and produced a 34-page special report and wrote 'it (Network Marketing) finally looks set to come into its own here, in its third decade.'

Network Marketing offers many things to many people. From £100 per month for a few luxuries to £100,000 per month mega-incomes. What most people find difficult is committing themselves to learning this profession. This is mainly because they feel insecure about the future of the industry and their potential within it. Network Marketing is new; it has had some dark times and corrupt operators. It is not well known and often misunderstood. If people knew what I now know, I am sure that they would spend the time necessary to become competent and successful.

This book is simple as are the reasons why Network Marketing will boom in the UK and Europe. They come down to what I call the 'Three and Five'. Network Marketing is being driven by three major trends and five key growth factors. They are now in place for it to boom. This book explains the 'Three and Five' so everyone will know the facts in a simple and logical way.

To complete the explanation, I will make some growth forecasts for the UK and Europe and explain some of the key aspects of the business. I will focus on the UK though the comments I make are just as relevant overseas, especially in Europe, where I have made presentations in many countries.

To start any new business most people need solid information on the industry they are entering. To put heart and soul into Network Marketing, you may need to question the 'why' behind this fascinating industry before the 'how'. More importantly, the industry has been around for 40 years so why join or get more actively involved now? You will need 'The Big Picture'.

I will often use the terms 'we' meaning 'those of us in Network Marketing'. I will also use 'he' or 'him': I am not being sexist. It just helps me to get away from the he/she confusion. Actually, given the significant success of women in Network Marketing, it would not hurt slanting the grammar men's way to give them a hand.

There is overwhelming evidence that Network Marketing is now destined for dramatic growth. I make no excuses about my enthusiasm, I'm very excited about my involvement in this industry. And this is why.

I hope you enjoy this book.

Edward.

Contents

CHAPTER 1

What is Network Marketing?
Magic Formula
Right Place - Trendsurfing
Right Time - Industry Business Cycle

CHAPTER 2

Primary Trend 1 - Lifestyle

CHAPTER 3

Primary Trend 2 - Self-employment

CHAPTER 4

Primary Trend 3 - Direct Shopping

CHAPTER 5

Right Time - Boom Time
Quick History Lesson
Five Factors:
Growth Factor 1 - Successful systems
Growth Factor 2 - Sufficient numbers
Growth Factor 3 - Regulatory Environment
Growth Factor 4 - Positive media image
Growth Factor 5 - Success overseas
Further factors

CHAPTER 6

Predictions for the future
Summary

CHAPTER 7

Key Points on Network Marketing
Pyramid Sales
The Saturation myth
The Real power of Network Marketing
Get Rich Quick Schemes
How an income grows
Notes for readers outside the UK

What is Network Marketing?

Network Marketing, sometimes called Multi-Level Marketing, or MLM, is a method of distributing consumer goods. Instead of selling through shops, a Network Marketing company offers the opportunity for Self-Employed people, called 'distributors' or 'consultants', to sell the products directly to customers. To grow their business, distributors are also offered the opportunity of developing a network of distributors on which they can earn commissions on their team's sales.

These commissions are called **'bonuses'** or **'royalties'** and to the Network Marketing companies, they are the cost of growth. To the distributors, bonuses are the major profit centre changing a Network Marketing opportunity from a linear income, like a salesperson, into a *BUSINESS* with on-going residual incomes similar to those received by recording artists or authors.

> ## To the distributors, bonuses are the major profit centre

This Business creates the opportunity for very large incomes which is why so many already successful business people and professionals are joining the industry. That said, the vast majority of distributors are looking to earn only a few hundred pounds to increase their lifestyle.

Your Network of Business Partners

The Magic Formula

Bill Gates, of Windows and Microsoft fame, is the richest man in the USA with a £10 billion fortune. He is three to four times richer than anyone in the UK and he had made his fortune by his early forties. So how did he make so much money so quickly?

He wasn't in the computer software business when it started. He wasn't even born when it started.

He isn't that much brighter than you or I.

He doesn't work that much harder than you or I.

He didn't start with lots of money. He set up in his garage.

He has been so successful because he was in the **right place** at the **right time** and took massive action. He joined the computer software industry as it started to boom.

Anita Roddick of Body Shop fame was the same. She joined the Natural Cosmetics and Franchising industries at the right time and shot to fame and fortune.

**Entrepreneurs have a Magic Formula
that everyone can follow.
Be in the Right Place at the Right Time**

Right Place

Trendsurfing

*'A fad is a wave in the ocean, and a trend is the tide. A fad gets
a lot of hype, and a trend gets very little.
Like a wave a fad is very visible, but is goes up and down in a
big hurry. Like the tide, a trend is almost invisible, but it's very
powerful over the long term'*

'The 22 Immutable Laws of Marketing', Reis and Trout

Industries with the biggest futures are those positioned ahead of the strongest trends, which I call Primary Trends. Primary Trends are so fundamental and powerful that they are often referred to as Revolutions: The Information Revolution, The Learning Revolution, The Socialist Revolution.

For Network Marketing to be a major growth industry of the future it needs to be driven by Primary Trends.

Primary Trends are mainly found in three key areas. They are:

1. What makes people happy.
2. How people make money.
3. The economy.

I will explain what is happening in each area and what the Primary Trends are, in fact, they will quickly reveal themselves. Obviously, the three primary trends are behind Network Marketing or I wouldn't be writing this book. They will confirm the 'Right Place' element of the entrepreneur's magic formula.

*A trend is a direction that a lot of consumers, the leading-edge
consumers, are taking-the general drift of the marketplace.
Trends are important if you want to position a product (or yourself) in the market and appeal to people in the language they are
now or will be taking.*

'The Popcorn Report', Faith Popcorn

Right Time
The Industry Business cycle

Successful entrepreneurs know that all industries go through what are called 'Business Cycles'. A business cycle splits into different phases called *Development, Growth, Maturity and Renewal.*

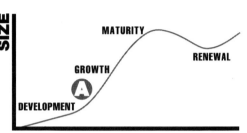

- **Development** phase is for pioneers, and only a few survive as companies have to develop the products that sell and devise systems that succeed in each market. This is the most difficult phase and only the most determined profit.

- **Growth** phase is when companies are in 'overdrive' and times are good for many involved. The hard work in establishing a recognised industry has been done and the momentum created.

- **Maturity** phase is where most people tend to join industries because it is 'safe', accepted and stable.

- **Renewal** phase is when new ideas, systems and technology enter the industry. This starts another Development phase of the next business cycle.

The best time to join any industry is at the start of the Growth phase of a business cycle (Point A). Network Marketing in the United Kingdom has just entered the Growth phase of its first business cycle.

The business world is changing so quickly that it is not just the entrepreneurs who need to ensure they pick the right industries to be in. Technology and the global market have meant that all jobs and businesses are constantly under threat so you need to know that you are in an 'on trend' industry at the right time.

If you join a new industry too early you will be Pioneering. You will probably receive a lot of negative comment and most people fail as systems are unproven. Fortunately for you and me, in all business cycles key 'Growth Factors' eventually slot into place and the industry booms.

Today's rapidly changing market means that, whether you are looking for a part-time income or a new full-time career, you must pick your industries well. So pick 'the right place' by examining the current major trends in society and 'the right time' by determining the right Growth factors.

Primary Trend #1
What's important in life?

Lifestyle Revolution

The motivation behind all of our behaviour is the pursuit of happiness. Faith Popcorn, arguably the world's leading trend-spotter, conducts her primary research by asking this simple question ...

> ### Are you happy?

She finds that this question opens the flood gates to what people really think and feel. To answer they reveal their inner-most concerns and desires that will drive their behaviour in the future.

Are you happy with your income?
Are you happy with your home?
Are you happy with your relationships?
Are you happy with your security?
Are you happy with yourself?

Ask yourself some 'Are you happy?' questions.

The fact is that most people are unhappy with their life. After spending so much time madly working during the 1980's to pay for that better house, better car and foreign holiday, few feel wealthier. Economists can prove we are financially wealthier but they cannot measure the poverty of the soul.

Feeling unfulfilled is a major trend. People are giving up excellent salaries in the cities to move to towns and places where they take less demanding jobs to 'spend time with the family' or 'for a better quality of life'. People are taking jobs where they get more 'personal satisfaction', or 'personal freedom' and are starting their own businesses because 'they always wanted to'. We want flexibility and substance in our life.

The personality cult of glamour and fame is finally slowly dying as we realise how shallow that existence is. Character traits of honesty, integrity and trust are becoming important again as they offer the only solution to long term happiness and self-esteem. Looking good is no replacement for feeling good. People in general want a better life and they want a better lifestyle.

To reinforce this you will find, in the first pages of nearly every economic textbook what economists call the 'basic economic problem'.

> *'Human existence has been preoccupied with the production and consumption of wealth, the desire for which seems to arise from man's basic impulse to increase his lifestyle (my word). The concepts of wealth and lifestyle, therefore, stand at the heart of economics.'*
>
> **Hardwick, Khan and Mead,**
> **An Introduction to Modern Economics, Longman, 1992.**

Wealth is cars, houses, money, businesses and the other things you buy and own.

Lifestyle is the enjoyment you get from these things and how you live your life around them.

There is a limit to our time and effort. Depending on our aspirations, we focus on either Wealth or Lifestyle. We focus on what is important to us at the time.

After World War 2 we were poor and so we focused on creating wealth. Having a great lifestyle was not a priority. We advanced so rapidly that by the 1960's we decided to enjoy ourselves, hence the 'swinging sixties'. Life was so good, that we were unprepared for the oil and business shocks of the 1970's. This resulted in new national leaders who promised wealth with stability. Leaders such as Thatcher, Kohl, Mitterand, Reagan and Nakasome sang a song of expansion, economic efficiency and financial opportunity. They pointed the way to 'true capitalism' and society became fixated on wealth creation whatever the cost.

The eager 1980's

'He who dies with the most toys wins.' **Car sticker**

The 1980's saw the dawn of the new Information Age. Service sectors such as PR, banking, publishing, computing and advertising exploded into activity. A return to economic strength was reflected in the booming stock and property markets. We bought houses, cars, shares and other assets. With new technology such as fibre optics and the silicon chip, this era made us richer, faster than ever before. Inefficient and uncompetitive industries faltered and business cycles which used to take 20 years took only 5 years as technology speeded up the world. These were exciting times.

The bubble finally burst, bringing many people back to earth. Following the quagmire of recession and unemployment, many are analysing whether this 'rush for money' made them happy. We have started to look again for quality of life. Relationships and spirituality are being discussed openly again. The 'nineties' caring man' has been born and 'sixties' clothes and music are back in fashion. Welcome to the Lifestyle Revolution.

The Lifestyle Revolution

If you doubt the coming of the Lifestyle Revolution, you only have to look as far as the High Street. The 1960's are back. Platform shoes, miniskirts, psychedelic rock, 'granny glasses', flares and love beads are in fashion. The Beatles are back in the music charts and they have even run the Woodstock Music concert again!

New technology and communications will make the swing towards Lifestyle faster and stronger and create more momentum than any previous swing in history. Lifestyle is the new focus, so creating better Lifestyle is a major trend in society. It is so powerful that it has become a Primary Trend.

Network Marketing is in the forefront of the Lifestyle Revolution. You work when you like, where you like, as much as you like. It is completely flexible and works around you. It is also based on you making other people successful, whilst encouraging you to work on your own personal development. The Lifestyle Revolution is driving Network Marketing and anyone involved with it forward.

> ***Network Marketing is in front of the Lifestyle Revolution. You work when you like, where you like, as much as you like***

Primary Trend #2
How do we make money?

The Self-employment Revolution

The Income Paradigm.

When it comes to making money, most people have what is called a *Job Paradigm*. A paradigm is the way you view a certain situation. The *Job Paradigm* is that you think that making money is based on having a 'good job'. This is now a dangerous view of making money because the world of work has changed forever and many jobs are under threat.

Today, you need an *Income Paradigm*. Instead of your focus being on a job, you need to look for opportunities to make an income. It is time to drop the blind allegiance to the sacred Job. The 'Job' has changed and it does not mean what it used to. Unfortunately for most of us, to reject the job paradigm is difficult because in the past it was the answer to long term happiness.

 The 'Job' has changed and it does not mean what it used to.

Are you a Dumb Frog ?

They say, if you drop a frog into a pot of hot water, it'll hop right out (smart frog).

Yet, if you put the frog into a pot of cold water first, then by applying heat, bring the water to the boil, the frog will happily stay there until it dies. (dumb frog)

Many people are currently thinking and acting like that dumb frog. The problem lies with the 'job paradigm' which assumes that a job is a source income with long term security and many other benefits. Now that things have changed, the gas has been turned up under 'their pot'.

We spend years at schools, colleges and, for a few, University, to gain skills for life, more importantly, to get a 'good job'. People are ranked by their job. Parents push their children 'to get a job'. When political parties talk about improving people's lives, they talk about jobs.

The reason is that in the past a job proved itself to be a stable source of income which gave you a better life. The better the job, the better the income, the better the life. You could rely on it, you had long term security. Some industries like steel, mining, ship building and government service took it further and a job became a 'Job for Life'. It also provided opportunities for promotion and other non-financial benefits, such as a sense of community, identity, challenge, achievement and growth.

Our **Job Paradigm** became...

Job = Income *plus*
    a Promise of Security *plus*
    a Promise of further Opportunities *plus*
    Other Benefits

For these additional promises and benefits, we put up with domineering bosses, unpaid overtime, discrimination , being told what to wear, when to work, when to turn up and when to go on holiday, etc., etc. We delegated the responsibility for much of our lives to our employer on the understanding that they would look after us.

Welcome to the Information Age

We are now in the Information Age of new technology and global markets. These twin forces have changed the world forever and as communications get faster, so does the change. There is no going back.

Technology and global markets have improved our lives in many ways. They have also destroyed the unwritten 'job promise' forever. Many of us feel 'let down' by organisations and the government because they have broken their job promises. The reality is that they were promises they would never be able to keep anyway.

In today's markets, companies have to be more efficient in everything, especially the labour-force. Labour is now a global market so employees in Manchester have to compete with those in Malaysia. Productivity is the watchword - it refers to 'How much an employee produces and at what cost'. If employees cannot be competitively productive then their company will make that person/team/division/factory redundant and find a more efficient solution.

If unions think they are going to fight that economic reality, then they are dreaming. We can see them trying in Germany and France but they are only delaying the inevitable. Employers have little choice; they are competitive or they die. The economic disasters of Eastern Europe are a classic example of what happens if you try to fight the global market.

> *Many of us feel 'let down' by organisations and the government because they have broken their promises. The reality is that they were promises they would never be able to keep anyway.*

Promise of Job Security

Security is one of our primary needs for which other things are forsaken such as excitement, personal growth, recognition and respect. So powerful is the need for security, that it was natural to want a job because it subconsciously promised to provide that security. Today companies cannot offer income security to anyone and it is grossly incorrect to assume that they can.

Promise of further Opportunities

Promotion used to be part and parcel of a job so long as you performed and 'your face fitted'. In some organisations the whole concept of promotion was based on how long you had been with the company, as opposed to your competence and productivity. This was especially true in heavily unionised organisations, like the docks, steel mills and government organisations like the Army.

In a world of tightening budgets and 'flat' organisations, companies do not and cannot offer guaranteed promotion. Some companies now have only four levels from Board room to shop floor. The challenge and achievement of 'climbing the ladder' is dead.

Other Benefits

A job also offered many people the feeling of belonging and identity. People wear the companies they work for, or their profession, like a label. They proudly state 'I work for Ford', 'She works for British Telecom' or '20 years in the Army'. These statements impress people. They could be poorly paid, overworked, overstressed and poorly managed but 'they worked for XYZ PLC'.

In the new economic world, I feel sorry for someone who has a job with these big organisations because many are living under the shadow of redundancy. Sadly, millions have already been made redundant.

Professor Handy, the internationally renowned business guru calls this time 'The Age of Unreason' and suggests that the way we make our money in the future will be very different from the past. In short, a new paradigm. If you want security, development opportunities, challenge, achievement and increasing benefits do not look to the job world.

In the new economic world, companies are having to:

1. Pay more for high tech, high value employees.

2. Pay everyone else less.

3. Replace people, especially management, administration and manual labour workers with new technology.

4. Employ part-time or contract workers who do not have the same social commitments as far as redundancy, training, pension, sick pay and holidays.

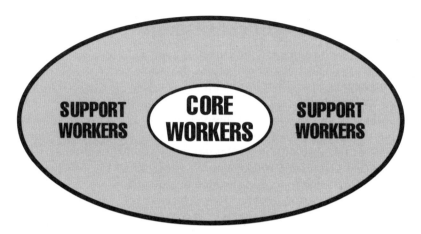

This ongoing and inevitable process is creating two types of employees:

1. Core Workers are those employees who could be considered assets of a company. They are the people who hold the valuable 'people element' of a company like important client relationships, specific skills or abilities.

These valuable employees will have more pay, more responsibilities and more stress. Weekly, we read reports saying that the workload is getting too much for UK workers and management. Stress is increasing, seriously affecting the health and lifestyle of many Core Workers.

When you relate this to the Lifestyle trend, you can see why so many core workers and professionals are looking for ways to get out of the 'Rat Race' and to have a better Lifestyle.

> **'If you win the Rat Race, you are still a Rat'**
> **Lilly Tomlin**

2. Support Workers are not vital to the company.

Support workers make up the bulk of most companies as they fill the ranks of management, administration, finance, manufacturing, service and other systemised areas. They are the real victims of this change in business. It is their wages and positions which are being slashed. They are being made redundant in droves or hired on a contract or seasonal basis. As they hold general skills, they needed the job security more than the average 'Core Worker'. They are the ones who wanted to hold the 'job paradigm' as true. They are the ones who will feel the most let down as it is destroyed.

Complete Structural Change

Technology and the global markets are changing the complete structure of the labour market which in turn, will change the way we live. It's not just the loss of job security and opportunities, these structural changes affect what education we feel we need, where we need to live and many other things.

One thing is for sure, the 21st Century will be very different from the 20th. To enjoy the future, we need to understand and accept the changing world. This allows us to take back the responsibility we subconsciously delegated to governments and companies to take control of our lives. To reinforce these comments, here are some supporting economic observations:

> *Technology and the global markets are changing the complete structure of the labour market which in turn, will change the way we live.*

Not changing is very expensive.

When companies and governments bury their heads in the sand and refuse to change they just delay the inevitable, making any changes more dramatic and painful for everyone. General Motors didn't change fast enough and lost over £15 billion in one year! British Telecom has laid off 100,000 employees, at a cost of £700 million in 1995 alone.

No large industry is safe.

Even the safe, secure UK banking industry is under fire with 90,000 redundancies and Chief Executives predicting another 50,000.

No 'Jobs for Life.

Even the 'protected' employment environments, such as government service, armed forces and unionised labour, have lost the 'job for life' as governments have had to tighten budgets. Unfortunately, these people have less of the skills necessary to make a bright future in the modern world.

Redundancies have only just started.

In Europe, companies and government organisations in relative terms have only just started mass redundancies compared to North American operations who started these 'rationalisation' programmes years ago. Millions of jobs will be shed. This makes grim reading when you consider that unemployment in the EC is already running at 10%. Spain is currently 24%! Germany's unemployment rate tops 4 million and France is in turmoil.

Huge Under-Employment.

Unemployment figures are a scam as they do not include the millions of people, of all ages, on training schemes, unregistered for benefit, on part-time work or on low pensions. These people are the under-employed and are often the real casualties of the changing work place.

Why Rehire?

Even if the economy gets stronger, large organisations are not going to rehire workers in their masses as they are now well aware of the costs of redundancy. Re-employment will be on a part-time or contract basis.

Part-time, Low Paid, Low Skills Jobs.

For Support Workers, the new jobs are mainly low paid, low skilled and part-time, which are so aptly called 'McJobs'. In fact, according to Businessweek magazine, a staggering 90% of new jobs in the UK are part-time.

Manufacturing and service businesses are relocating to low wage areas where they employ low paid workers to work on computers, telephones and construction lines. Korea is proud to announce massive investment in the UK. Why? Because some UK workers are now cheaper than Koreans. I have nothing against Koreans, but how is it that the British worker is now worth less than a Korean worker?

More Competition For Jobs.

The unemployed and under-employed will also have to compete with increasing numbers of housewives, school leavers, and retired people looking for work. These people and those in 'training schemes' are rarely counted in the employment figures, however they number millions.

Over 40s Are Over The Hill.

Another rapidly rising trend is forced redundancies for the over 40s. The UK Institute of Employment Consultants report that 75% of employers want candidates between 21-30 and 60% of them specify age limits. The over 50's are the least desired with 419,000 between 50 -64 registered as unemployed. Employers see them as over-qualified and over-priced.

Rich Are Getting Richer.

And the poor poorer. The gap between the incomes of rich (the top 20% of incomes) and the poor (the bottom 20%) has continued to widen. In the 1970's the rich's income was on average four times that of the poor. Now it is seven times. The average household income of the bottom 40% is only £6,023.

Living Longer

What makes these realities uglier is that most people will live longer, with the chances being that you will live until you are 70, 80 or 90 years old. People could have to live 10 to 30 years without strong cashflow and valued employment. The humiliation of poverty will visit increasing numbers.

The Real Timebomb

As if the death of job security and opportunities isn't enough, the real timebomb is pensions. A statement on pensions from the latest Institute for Public Policy Research report says it all ....

> *'The present system is unsatisfactory for many people. Those who are low-paid, part-time, casual, mobile, Self-Employed, working for small firms or who have interrupted work histories owing to home responsibilities, unemployment, sickness or disability are more likely to be poor in old age'*

In other words, if you are not in the exclusive group of Core Workers, they predict you are very likely to spend many years of your life in poverty. And they do mean poverty.

'Which Pension' magazine reported that by 2030 the state pension will be just 8.5% of the national average male income, a little over £35 in today's money. Other reputable sources report that the average occupational pension will be only £30.53 a week after tax. Who can live on that? What about food, house repairs, holidays, gifts or emergencies?

> *This is a national crisis so large that most politicians refuse to confront it.*

Governments cannot afford to pay for pensions in the future without tax rates exceeding 75% and that is not going to happen.

The only way for you to protect yourself is to build additional pension provisions. Most people are going to have to find another income source quickly or accept being poor for a very long time.

A New Paradigm

Forget the job paradigm. The only viable view on making money is an **INCOME paradigm.** Your focus should be 'how am I going to earn an income?' not 'where am I going to get a job?'. This new view on life should allow you to assess the potential of any job, business or educational opportunity in a realistic light.

Millions of people will need a new income for many reasons and many are being left in the cold by the Job or Employment market. They are therefore, forced to investigate **Self-Employment** in order to secure an income. **The movement toward self-employment is the next PRIMARY trend** which focuses on 'How We Make Money'.

Self-employment challenges

Most Support Workers who are looking to self-employment for an income do not have the financial resources, small business knowledge or saleable skills to be a success. Many will try to own small businesses or become consultants, however the vast majority of these ventures fail to deliver sufficient profit fast enough. It is not surprising to know that 80% of new businesses ventures fail within the first 2 years.

Unless they want to work as cleaners or commission-only sales people, they will need some other form of income opportunity. In short they need a business where they don't have to have prior knowledge or skills to do it. A business where there is little capital investment involved and very low risk. A business where they are helped and supported as they learn and develop their livelihood.

Basically, what we are describing here is some sort of low cost franchise. A franchise that anyone can do, where everyone has a good chance of making money related to the time and effort they expend. A 'People's Franchise'.

To assist the millions of Support Workers, this People's Franchise must not discriminate against anyone. Neither age, physical health, location, sex, experience skills nor capital investment must stop anyone from succeeding.

The 'People's Franchise

Network Marketing is the only industry that offers a 'People's Franchise'. It is a new key industry and sits well in front of the PRIMARY trend towards self-employment. Self-employment is accelerating around the world as large groups of people continue to be excluded from the 'job' market. To them Network Marketing is a very attractive option.

The worst hit groups are those over forty, women, ethnic minorities and the disabled. When you consider that these four groups make up over 80% of the population, you can appreciate how powerful this Primary Trend is becoming and how exciting the prospects for Network Marketing are.

Network Marketing is the only industry that offers a 'People's Franchise'

Small Point for the employed.

Self-employment is fantastic. In fact, most people who work for themselves say they could never work for anyone else again. Recommendations cannot come any stronger than that. Imagine the security of no-one sacking you and earning what you are worth for once.

Self-Employed Alternatives

The move to being Self-Employed will be a shock for many people. At the very least they can prepare themselves by understanding what options are available to them. Anyone investigating the Self-employment market needs to analyse each opportunity against capital and skills required, a risk/reward ratio and the level of lifestyle they will have. Network Marketing comes out as the clear leader. You can see why when we look at the other options;

Manual labour. Everyone has a high chance of succeeding at carrying bricks, waiting at tables, making beds or cleaning loos. With no risk and poor rewards, the lifestyle element is zero. An option certainly, but no thanks.

Commission-only sales is up-market manual labour. Potential income is high for the tiny amount of people who succeed. Not for the average person who wants to stay sane.

Consultancy has the perfect combination of low risk, high rewards and lifestyle. It is fantastic for the 0.001% of the population who can find enough clients to pay enough for their skills so that they can make a living.

Starting your own business is the first thought in this 'nation of shopkeepers'. The reality of high risks, low financial rewards and a terrible lifestyle should turn warning lights on. With a quoted 80% failure rate in the first few years, you must be brave, smart and mad.

Buying a franchise is a good option as it combines the freedom of owning your own business with some security of working with a larger company. Few franchisees fail but often you have the same lifestyle limitations as owning your business. Good Franchise companies are very selective about candidates, however the large financial investment needed to set up a franchise puts most people off anyway.

Network Marketing offers a franchise at a fraction of the cost. The rewards are unlimited depending on how much work you put in and the size of the network you build. The lifestyle aspect is probably the best thing about Networking because you have complete control over when you work and how much you work.

Primary Trend #3
Opportunities in the Economy

Direct Shopping Revolution

The last Primary Trend we shall look at is an economic trend. It centres on the changing buying patterns of the consumer; instead of going to a shop we can now buy from the comfort of our own homes. This is the age of Direct Shopping and it is absolutely fundamental to the growth of Network Marketing.

Consumer goods are the key product to be involved in whether you are making the product or distributing it. Manufacturing is making things while distribution is about getting the finished goods to the customer. Manufacturing used to be the growth side of the business, now it is distribution. U.S. Professor Paul Pilzer in his book '*Should you quit before you are fired*' explains why:

> In the 1960's, the manufacturing proportion of a product's final price was typically about 50%, with distribution the other 50%. If the product cost $300, the manufacturing cost would be $150.
>
> If the manufacturer made a 20% saving ($30) through new technology then he could reduce the price by $30 or keep the $30 as additional profits. These were attractive savings and this promoted the increased use of new technology.
>
> Today, that $300 product's price has probably dropped to about $100 and, more importantly, the manufactured proportion of the final price would be no more than 20%, more likely 10%. If the manufacturer applied new methods now and made a 20% saving, they'd reduce the price by only $4. On the other hand, a 20% saving applied to distribution would reduce the price by $16. Four times the profit for the same percentage improvement. The opportunities for creating wealth are in Distribution!
>
> | | 1960's | | 1990's | |
> |---|---|---|---|---|
> | *Selling Price* | $300 | 20% saving | $100 | 20% saving |
> | *Manufacturing* | *50%* | $30 | 20% | $4 |
> | *Distribution* | *50%* | $30 | 80% | $16 |

Now we're cocooning for our lives. **Paris Metro 1991**

Faith Popcorn, in her best selling book on trends, The Popcorn Report, explains that one of the major trends in the 1990's is what she calls 'cocooning'. 'Cocooning' is about people retreating to their home 'cocoon' because the outside world is scary, violent and confusing - whereas the home is warm and safe. In reaction to this trend, she states;

> **'distribution will be the next consumer oriented revolution. Direct shopping from the producer to you - bypassing the retailer altogether, no middlemen, no stops along the way.'**
>
> **The Popcorn Report**

Manufacturers have two ways of distributing products:

- ● **Retailing (customer to the shop)** *or*
- ● **Direct Shopping (shop to the customer)**

Faith Popcorn claims that Direct Shopping will be the business to be in. It is a simple process to work out why. The manufacturer and the customer are the two important bodies in the economic process, with the customer as king. Manufacturers must choose their means of distribution well to ensure they are best able to satisfy the consuming publics needs.

The Customer is King

Technology has now meant that consumer goods' manufacturers can produce an unlimited array of products, all in differing varieties, brands and models. We have never had so many choices. Add to that, the supermarket and chemist chain's 'own brand' products plus increasing global imports and we have achieved the great marketing dilemma; an increasingly **confused consumer**. Consumers like to make informed buying decisions but, with so many choices on offer, this can prove a little taxing. The successful companies of the future will be the ones which can **educate the public the most effectively about their products.**

Consumers will always want a more convenient way of shopping whilst getting a 'good deal'. They expect shopping to get easier and become more enjoyable, with better value products every year. They are in the driving seat and know it.

Challenged Manufacturers

In days of old the manufacturers had the power. They spent the advertising money, they owned the brands. They controlled the consumers with supermarkets, department stores and shops acting as a supply chain to hungry consumers.

Now the supply chain holds the power as manufacturers jockey for shelf space against the 'own brand' products of distributors. Sainsbury's, the supermarket chain, launched a cola product against the mighty Coca-Cola and Pepsi; within 3 years they had cornered 10% of the market. They achieved this without massive marketing budgets. These companies want and need to get back control or their brands will become irrelevant. In short, they need to by-pass traditional methods of distribution and supply direct to the customer.

Retailing

Most consumer products are distributed through retail outlets. The challenge for the retailing sector is increased competition, rapid market changes and a disinterested, financially concerned public.

There has been a revolution in retailing where friendly, helpful high street and corner shops been replaced by retail chains, like Boots, Dixons, W.H.Smiths, Rymans and McDonalds. They are slugging it out with 'out of town' shopping malls, retail parks, warehouses and discount clubs. These are signs of a mature industry controlled by giant companies who spend millions enticing customers into their shops. Big retail organisations now control the access to the customers and hold the manufacturers to ransom.

The retail pie is barely growing so for the giants to continue to grow, they must take a slice from their competitors and cut costs. The main victims are the small retail shops, which are dying in their thousands. Staff are being laid off in their tens of thousands. Those left over are barely paid enough to motivate them to serve and educate the customer. As competition increases, prices decline and so does quality. It is a spiral that will be the undoing of many retailers as the customer is not truly winning in this process.

This is not the industry of the future as neither the manufacturers nor the customers are winning. Retailing does not address the 'cocooning' trend. Customers will go elsewhere if offered a better alternative.

Direct Shopping

Direct Shopping is the distribution alternative to retailing and it can be split into two forms;

1. **Direct Marketing, and**
2. **Direct Selling.**

The difference between the two is that in Direct Selling, the company uses people to make sales face to face and in Direct Marketing the company uses media such as magazines, newspapers, leaflets, direct mail, computers, catalogues and television.

Direct Marketing

Computer systems and new communications have allowed Direct Marketing companies to by-pass the retailer effectively and efficiently and this industry boomed in the 1980's. The convenience of shopping by mail or phone has mass appeal. This sector will continue to diversify and expand rapidly as new forms of communications, electronic banking and more efficient home delivery improve the service.

The Archilles Heel of Direct Marketing is its lack of human contact, face to face product explanation and demonstration. It is also becoming an extremely competitive market which means that the consumer is becoming increasingly bombarded with advertising and customer prospecting; this, in turn, reduces effectiveness and increases costs.

There are few opportunities for the Self-Employed masses in this industry as it becomes increasingly sophisticated and capital-intensive. Small mail order businesses rarely produce sensible incomes given the effort put in. Envelope stuffing and telesales are not really considered options for a long term lifestyle change.

Direct Selling

Direct Selling is normally seen as the 'down market' cousin of all forms of distribution. Here, the shop is taken to the customer by a *Self-Employed* salesperson. The product is explained, demonstrated and sold to the customer, often in the home.

Direct Selling is a relatively small method of distribution compared with Retailing and Direct Marketing but offers huge expansion possibilities as it is now attractive to customers, manufacturers and participants alike.

Customers win

The customer benefits enormously. Firstly, the convenience of the shop coming to the home. Secondly, professional education on the products. Finally, a personal after sales service. The customer also buys from someone who actually uses the product so the immense power of 'word-of-mouth' advertising comes into play. No other form of distribution even comes close in these areas and companies are continually improving their service standards and guarantees.

Manufacturers win

Direct Sales is a manufacturer's dream because their product is taken directly to the customer's home. The customer is **educated** on their product alone. The manufacturer also gets customer and product sales information much faster as they become much 'closer' to the customer. They have gained back some control. As sales staff are remunerated on a "commission only" sales basis, they are much more motivated to succeed.

Participants win

New technology, products and remuneration systems means the business has changed, thus increasing the rewards and the chances of success.

It's a win-win situation for everyone!

Direct Selling offers the best win-win situation for all elements in the economic chain. Other forms of distribution are not fulfilling the changing needs of the producer or the customer and, inevitably, those guys decide the rules of the Distribution game. The timing has not been right for Direct Selling to come into the limelight until now. It's only now that we have busier lives, job insecurity, a competitive global market and new technology that makes this kind of distribution able to compete with retailing and Direct Marketing.

Direct Selling has changed significantly in the last 20 years as new technology and techniques have vastly increased its potential for growth. Behind the scenes, the ugly sister of distribution has been having a dramatic makeover. Gone are the 'foot-in-the-door' salesmen. The Cinderella of the Direct Shopping Revolution has joined the party in the shape of Network Marketing. Direct Selling is split into two categories;

1. Single level - *Person to Person or Party Plan*
2. Multi-level - *Network Marketing*

'Single level' means that the direct sales people are only paid on their own personal sales. 'Multi-level' means that the direct salespeople, called 'Distributors' or 'Consultants', are paid on their own sales AND royalties on the sales of a set number of levels of recruits in their network.

The essential difference between the two categories is how a company seeks to grow. Single level direct sales companies want to maintain control over the field leadership, recruitment and training and growth. Network Marketing companies subcontract these roles to their distributors, making them responsible for growth. It is this opportunity to grow the number of people in the business that offers the big money and creates the dynamism of Network Marketing. This is the reason why Network Marketing is growing so much faster than its single level friends.

The People's Franchise

There are three primary trends in society today that are fundamental to Network Marketing:

The Lifestyle Revolution

The Self-employment Revolution

● The Direct Shopping Revolution

Only one industry, Network Marketing, sits in front of all three 'revolutions'. It is the only growth business which offers the average person opportunity, security and many other non-financial benefits. It truly is 'The People's Franchise'. It is not some revolutionary form of business. It is a method of distributing consumer products which has developed over time so that it is 'the right place' to be for people looking for an income.

Network Marketing's friend - Technology

Network Marketing's greatest friend is technology and the change that it creates.

Technology has created so much wealth that we are now focusing on Lifestyle to make us happy.

Technology has destroyed the established paradigm of job security and opportunities.

Technology has thrown up distribution as the business to be revolutionised next.

Technology has allowed Network Marketing to grow through its compensation plan.

In today's changing world, I would prefer to have technology and change as my partners, rather than my enemies.

Right Time – Boom Time

The *Trend Journal* said it all...

'Timing is everything'

Smart businessmen rarely join an industry at its birth. They join after the major mistakes have been made, at the start of the Growth phase.

The early days of an industry, the Development phase, are for those bull headed, rhino-skinned pioneers who get a kick out of creating new opportunities. They are the bruisers, the self-starters, the visionaries who are prepared to take the knocks, the failures and the rejection. Many feel that they are pioneers but in reality much less than 1% of the population are prepared to be pioneers.

The tiny percentage of pioneers who make it to the growth stage often make a lot of money and they certainly deserve it. Fortunately, the real money and fun is to be had in the growth stage, not the pioneering stage. If you join at the start of the growth, phase you have just as much chance of making a fortune as those with 20 years pioneering experience.

In fact, often you are better prepared because you will not have years of ingrained bad habits that need to be unlearned in order to succeed.

Remember, Bill Gates of Microsoft and Steve Jobs of Apple didn't join the computer industry at its birth. They joined in the 1970's, just before the boom times of the 1980's and 1990's.

If you are one of the million people who have joined and left a Network Marketing opportunity in the UK over the past 10 years, now is the time to rejoin and take advantage of the opportunity you saw before and to re-ignite the knowledge and skills you learned. There are also hundreds of thousands of skilled ex-Direct Sales or Party Plan people who should now investigate the new age of Network Marketing. These people do have an edge, if they are prepared to learn the new attitudes and skills. It would be a smart move.

Boom Time occurs in an industry when it enters the Growth phase of a business cycle. Obviously the most dramatic and exciting Growth phase is an industry's first one. This is because Growth rates and changes in the industry are more dramatic as the industry goes from unknown to known.

The proof in the Boom Time of Network Marketing is held in an analysis of Network Marketing's closest business, Franchising. Franchising is like an older brother to Network Marketing. It, too, offers a Self-Employed opportunity based on a proven system. By examining Franchising's growth, we are able to find out what Growth Factors must be in place for Network Marketing to Boom.

You can determine if an industry has entered its Growth phase by determining whether certain critical Growth factors are in place. Without all of these factors being in place, an industry can never truly boom.

So what happened to Franchising?

Franchising entered the Growth phase of its first business cycle in the UK in the early 1980's. They finally had **five critical growth factors** in place and grew like wildfire.

Annual Gross Turnover (£bn) grew from £850 million in 1984 to £5,240 million in 1990. An incredible 600% growth! (and is still growing).

> ### *Franchising grew 600% in 6 years!*

The critical growth factors Franchising needed were:

1. **It had spent time as a 'fringe' form of business, building its reputation as its successful companies *fine-tuned their systems to the UK culture.***

2. **It had a *sufficient number of successful companies* to expand from.**

3. **It had a strengthening regulatory environment, including a strong *trade association* in the British Franchise Association.**

4. **It was developing an *increasingly positive media image.***

5. **It had *huge success overseas* to measure against.**

All of these factors are vital for sustainable long term growth of Franchising and also for Network Marketing. They are in priority order, as it is first vital that companies in the market develop their business to the personality of the nation and create a high success rate for committed operators.

'Business format franchising entered a dynamic new phase during the 1980's, mainly as a result of economic and political changes. In the early 1980's, the growth in unemployment created a vast pool of individuals all wishing to try out their entrepreneurial skills by setting up their own business.

The decline in the manufacturing sector has also led to a growing service-oriented economy which is conducive to business format franchising as it represents an <u>efficient and flexible distribution system for goods and services.</u>'

The Keynote Report on Franchising, 4th ed., 1991

As shown in previous chapters, similar conditions present for Franchising are here again yet technology and the global market place has created some differences and so they require a slightly different solution. Network Marketing is a similar business system to franchising designed to match the new conditions in the 1990's and beyond.

The Final Confirmation

The final confirmation of the potential of Network Marketing is to determine whether those five Growth Factors are in place for Network Marketing today.

We will quickly discuss all of these factors

Growth Factor 1 *Successful systems*
Growth Factor 2 *Sufficient numbers*
Growth Factor 3 *Regulatory Environment*
Growth Factor 4 *Positive media image*
Growth Factor 5 *Overseas Success*

A Quick History Lesson

Before we examine the Five Growth Factors, a quick history lesson is useful to explain how the Network marketing industry has developed. Network Marketing's history in the UK can be broken into two periods which I have named the 'Ages' of the Pioneer and the Professional;

The Pioneering Age

Network Marketing, like new marketing methods, started in the USA. In the 1940's, a company called Californian Vitamins first allowed its direct sales people also to recruit other sales people for a commission from their recruit's sales. This company prospered, eventually changing its name to Nutrilite. Two of Nutrilite's top salesmen soon formed The Amway Corporation which has become the largest Network Marketing company in the world, with annual sales of in excess £4 billion.

In the UK, the first company to have a multi-level payment structure under the umbrella of the Direct Selling Association was in 1970.

The 1980's saw new UK companies start up and others arrive from overseas. These companies continued to build on the slow growth of the late 1970's. Some of the new companies achieved spectacular growth, however most failed. Often the balance between recruiting, retailing and training was not maintained which meant a **high drop out rate** in many companies.

A number of people who failed in one company decided to 'have a go' at starting their own companies. These pioneers' companies were invariably **underfunded, poorly managed with poor retail opportunities.**

The industry was littered with failed fragrance, water filter, skin care and security companies. This 'me too' attitude did the industry little good, yet is normal for a new industry. It did make many people aware of the potential of the business and the importance of working with a stable, successful company. The industry did not receive positive media coverage because it did not deserve it.

All industries have growing pains. Network Marketing's major problem came in the form of its confusion with a concept called 'Pyramid Selling'. These scams are explained further on page 52. 'Pyramid Selling' is basically 'payment for the pure act of recruiting' and in 1973 Fair Trading laws were enacted to protect people from these pyramid sellers. Franchising was also caught in the public backlash .

Electronics, pharmaceuticals, cars, housing, oil, sport, even department stores have had their difficult times. Ours were in the 1970's, 1980's and early 1990's.

The Professional Age

In the early 1990's, a new breed of company emerged. These companies had learnt from observing the failures that professional management, adequate funding and a sound retail opportunity are vital building blocks to a successful Network Marketing company. Also that dramatic growth was no indication of long term success.

They focused heavily on making sure anyone could retail their products which is understandable given that the 'cowboy' companies around them didn't focus enough and had failed. These companies grew solidly whilst the 'cowboy' outfits either completely changed their business tactics or died. Most died.

These companies have been joined by very successful overseas companies to form a strong core from which the Network Marketing industry is now growing. The companies that survived the Pioneering Age are expanding across Europe. They have built strong foundations from which they are guaranteed to enjoy success in the coming years, making the previous years' performance pale into insignificance. Their stability and international income opportunity makes them a prime opportunity for today's entrepreneur. They will lead 'The Age of the Professional Network Marketer'.

The Profession of Networking

In this new age, it is clear that a new profession has developed just as the professions of lawyers, doctors, trainers, designers and pilots. The new Professional Networkers, most of whom are part-timers, have more knowledge, skills and attitudes than their forebears and set higher standards of professional conduct. They are also much more accepting of the actual time most people take to become a competent professional (patience is not a quality pioneers hold in abundance).

The new professionals have many obvious traits. Some of the major ones are:
- A zealous customer focus.
- An undying commitment to new distributor success.
- An acceptance of new Training and Development techniques.
- An openness to the media.
- An acceptance of considerable leadership development.
- A focus of competence development and lifetime learning.
- High use of technology.
- An international business view.
- Community based values.
- A long term business perspective.

GROWTH FACTORS

Growth Factor 1: *Successful systems*

Marketing and distribution businesses are highly dependent upon the cultures within which they operate. Just because a business works in North America does not necessarily mean it will work, without adjustment, in any other country. In fact, these businesses nearly always require adjustment to the local market and local culture. This proved to be true when American franchise systems were exported into the UK. Network Marketing companies had the same challenges. Unfortunately, pioneers are fairly stubborn people (that's what makes them good pioneers) and they often refused or ignored advice to change their business.

> **A great example of this concept is the McDonald's Corporation. McDonald's business system is the reason for its incredible success. Every McDonald's franchisor works 'the system' under pain of expulsion as they know it works. Yet go to Italy and pasta and wine are sold. Imagine what would happen if they wanted to sell wine from McDonald's in the USA! In Tokyo, they sell teriyaki. The same system with a twist to make it work in that country and its culture.**

The only true measure of successful business systems is durability. The UK now has a number of local and foreign companies which are 'UK adapted' and these companies are growing year on year. They are achieving activity and productivity levels of which the pioneering companies could only have dreamed. It wasn't until 1994/5 that most companies could truthfully claim they had a successful system.

Growth Factor 2: *Sufficient numbers*

One company is not an industry and all industries have proved that you need a small group to create the momentum necessary to create true growth and excitement. There are no standard measures but one would assume that at least twenty companies with multi-million pound turnover would be required in a country the size of the UK. This number was achieved by 1994.

Growth Factor 3: *Strong regulatory environment*

A strong regulatory environment is required by any industry so that unlawful operators can be prosecuted and consumers and junior participants protected.

Government legislation combats unethical operators on the fringes of the industry, trade associations regulate those operating in the main stream. Governments cannot effectively protect consumers or junior participants, as has been shown in countless industries such as insurance and financial services. Industries must police themselves.

Network Marketing has very strong laws governing it in the UK and will also soon have new legislation called Trading Schemes. This legislation, promoted by the industry leaders, will only assist the development of the business. It will also positively affect many other countries in Europe and beyond.

Following the Amway Corporation's legal success in 1979, it is often stated that a staggering 5 million people became Network Marketers in the USA. This would equate to 1 million in the UK and 7 million in Europe!

The Direct Selling Association represents and regulates the Network Marketing industry. It is becoming a stronger body and most companies operate under its DSA Code. The DSA's position has strengthened with increased media coverage and the growth of the industry.

Growth Factor 4: *Positive media image*

As a reaction to the unethical conduct of companies in earlier years, Network Marketing companies now **pride themselves on their level of ethics**. Their success combined with a pro-active trade association caused press coverage to improve. Since 1994 the media coverage has generally been excellent including two major reports by Business Age magazine, Britain's best selling business magazine and a regular column in the business pages of Evening Standard.

The continued improvement of media coverage will educate more people on the Network Marketing industry creating further business momentum.

Growth Factor 5: *Overseas success*

Observing how Network Marketing has developed in other countries should reveal what should happen in the UK and Europe. As with most new forms of marketing and distribution, Europe lags behind the rest of the developed world. Fortunately, it usually catches up quickly.

Reliable statistics are difficult to collate due to the unconsolidated nature of the industry and the preponderance of privately owned companies. The following estimates come from the most informed sources.

● **North America.** A latest 1995 statistics on the size of the US market is 7.2 million distributors! There are a number of companies with over 200,000 distributors! With a 250 million population, that equates to *2.4% of the population.* Canada's Network Marketing distributors account for the same percentage of the population as the industry booming in Mexico.

● **Australia.** The estimated number of distributors is 450,000 so, with a population just under 18 million, *that's 2.7% of the population.* **New Zealand** is believed to about the same.

● **South East Asia.** Estimates are difficult to find but Network Marketing has adapted extremely well to the Asian mentality because they are, like Europeans, natural Networkers of information and entrepreneurs. In some countries such as Taiwan, people claim that there are *10%* of the population involved! Some governments are pro-actively working with the industry. China will be the giant opportunity for many in that region, although there are many distribution challenges. With 600,000 joining in a couple of years, the potential is incredible.

● In **Japan,** companies have had incredible growth and collectively are estimated to involve *over 3% of the population.* The DSA reported a £19 billion annual turnover and Amway is one of the largest foreign companies. It seems as though the Japanese culture is perfectly suited to this industry.

● **South Africa** is catching up very quickly. If we took only the white population, there is *in excess of 2% involvement.* One company built a network of 50,000 in under 6 months! Now that the black and coloured populations will want to be more actively involved, one would expect rapid growth.

● **Central & Southern America,** we often hear of companies with tens of thousands of distributors. Again it suits the family networking temperament.

● Networking in the **Middle East** is already starting to grow and is bound to spread quickly around the Arab world. **Israel** has been a successful country for those who operate there.

● **India & Pakistan** will be huge Network Marketing countries. Distribution is a challenge but entrepreneurs will solve that.

● **Eastern Europe.** Eastern Europe has not been included in these predictions because of the scant information from there. Some companies have made significant inroads and are enjoying buoyant times. Hungary has reportedly over 100 companies and over 250,000 distributors involved. This area will continue to explode into activity due to its developing societies and the lack of opportunities for financial success of its people.

In all countries where Network Marketing is more developed than Europe, 2% of the population as independent distributors seems to be easily achieved. In the strong family based cultures of the East, 5% of the population could be reached. This bodes well for Europeans, as they also have very strong family links.

2% seems an easy target for Europe

As companies expand overseas, medium term opportunities for distributors in areas such as the Far East, South America, Eastern Europe and the Indian Continent look vast. 2% of the Indian sub-continent is 18 million people, China bares not even thinking about!

Additional growth factors

Apart from the key five growth factors, there are a few things that emphasise the perfect timing of Network Marketing in Europe and will help to drive the industry in the future.

1: Communications technology

Network Marketing is a business of communicating to people so anything that can speed up the process or make it more efficient will accelerate the growth. The increasing use of new communications technology, such as Voicemail, Teleconferencing, Fax Mail and private Satellite systems will drive Network Marketing into Europe. In the USA, they are commonplace tools of the trade. Who knows what the Internet will bring?

2: European integration

The more Europe works together, the faster success stories from other European countries will filter across borders raising the aspirations and activity of Networkers. Journalists will be exposed to more and more positive articles thus increasing the chances of more positive press. This has been the case in the UK.

3: Big name companies

Many major manufacturing multi-nationals are being led by their distributors such as supermarkets. They need new distribution outlets so will increasingly use Network Marketing. Their presence adds credibility and power to the industry, increasing government and media support.

Consumer goods giants such as Motorola, Panasonic, Gillette, Colgate-Palmolive, Microsoft, Compaq, MCI (British Telecom's US partner), US Sprint (French and Deutsche Telekom's US partner) and other high profile multi-nationals are already involved either directly or indirectly with Network Marketing.

It must be stated that Network Marketing is building its own multi-national consumer goods giants which will challenge and surpass many of the 'big' names of the past.

4: New country launches

Many established companies are expanding across national borders. The excitement of launching in new countries creates massive momentum for those companies. Companies have rapidly doubled, tripled and quadrupled their size through international expansion, so providing the answer to the limitless income growth claims of the industry.

Summary

All of the required Growth Factors are now in place for Network Marketing to boom in the UK. Four additional factors will only serve to accelerate the growth. Anyone involved or joining Network Marketing today can be certain that they truly are in the 'Right Place, at the Right Time.' All that remains for them is to learn the business and take massive action to exploit their good fortune, as you never know if you are ever going to be in this situation again.

To use the words of Winston Churchill...

'men occasionally stumble over the truth, but most pick themselves up and hurry off as if nothing happened'.

Don't hurry off before truly examining the potential of Network Marketing for you.

To put some numbers on the growth of Network Marketing, we have made the following predictions......

Predictions for the future

Current numbers

The actual numbers of total distributors and turnover for the UK and Western Europe are impossible to obtain. Best estimates for the number of distributors involved are 300,000 in the UK and 1 million in Western Europe. Turnover at retail prices less tax is estimated at £300 million for UK and £1 billion for Europe.

The United Kingdom

Using a 2% of population rule of thumb, the growth prediction will mean the UK industry should grow from 300,000 to 1.2 million distributors.

400% growth!!

The latest statistics from the DSA Research Unit showed that for 1994 the number of Network Marketing distributors grew by 38%. Early 1995 estimates show continued growth, estimated at over 35% per year. At this rate (say 35%), 1.2 million distributors will be reached by year 2000.

5 years!!

Currently average productivity is approx. £1,000 turnover per distributor per year. Given a new Professional Age with vastly enhanced Training & Development programs, communications technology and more effective Retail programs, average productivity is expected to increase by at least 50% over 5 years. This will create a minimum of £1.8 billion turnover by the year 2000.

600% growth in 5 years!!

From these predictions, you can see that the new Professional networkers will have significantly larger, active, productive and profitable networks. With more effective and durable networks, business builders should be able to extract at least 100% more profits.

> **'Network Marketing in the U.K. will involve 1.2 million people turning over £1.8 billion worth of products by the year 2000'.**

Europe

There are approximately 350 million people in Western Europe. With the **2% of the population** as distributors rule of thumb, we can reasonably expect *that 7 million people* will become involved. *__An extra 6 million people, or 600% growth!__*

Europeans are natural Networkers of information within families so you could expect the *growth rate to match the Asian figures of 4%* or more.

Any productivity gains in Europe are likely to be countered by restrictions imposed by government bureaucrats who must hate the concept of a free Self-Employed mass of people taking responsibility for their own lives. They will only help us when they realise that we hold the key to lowering unemployment rates through reclassifying these statistics as Self-Employed.

The current average turnover per distributor per year, approximately £1,000 or $1500, could stay the same and so I predict an *Annual Gross Turnover of at least $10 billion.*

The greatest challenges to European development are the highly regulated markets and archaic labour and business laws that hugely favour the completely outdated concept of the paternalistic government/big business state.

> *'Network Marketing in Europe will involve 7 million people turning over $10 billion worth of products by the year 2000'.*

There are good reasons to believe we will comfortably achieve much more than this considering new Direct Marketing techniques and technology, new product ranges and that many Direct Selling companies will take on Network Marketing's payment structure. For those who get involved now, **7 million people will come into the industry whether you introduce them or not.**

Eastern Europe has an additional 400 million people who are not going to be left out of the frame. Whenever a company starts in an Eastern European country, it is amazingly successful. I'm sure that 2%, or an additional 8 million people, will be involved rapidly. In fact, given a completely undeveloped distribution chain and limited economic opportunities for most people, this concept has a very large chance of taking firm root revealing 3%,5% or maybe 8% of the population involved. This concept is similar to the way mobile phones are booming in the Third World as the costs of laying telephone cable is too expensive.

The Major Benefit

All we've discussed are economics, logic, numbers and money. The reason for life is to feel good about yourself and others. The major benefit of Network Marketing is by far the Personal Growth element and Relationship gains. It is a particular focus of the industry and a major benefit to its participants.

If we could replace most people's income from their current job *and* give them the FREEDOM to earn more if they wanted to, work from home, spend more quality time with their family, increase their social life, reduce their stress, increase their travel and feel better about themselves; **everyone would consider joining.** Not by promising more money, just by giving them the chance to enjoy their life on what they've got. Most people don't care about earning great fortunes, they're more interested in enjoying life.

The self development side of Networking is my favourite area, as we see so many people, especially women, gain in confidence and self esteem. People gain the strength to make decisions which improve their lifestyle and those lives about them. No other industry does this on the scale of Network Marketing.

As people's belief in themselves grows, they change for the better and I've been privileged to see so much of this. Many people fear growth and what others may think. To them I say that everyone deserves to feel better about themselves and our business is based on doing just that.

Your Challenge

Carpe Diem - Seize the Day.

My challenge to you is to invest some more time in your future. I do not know what stage in your life this book has reached you. What I guarantee you is that the world you live in is changing at a pace few realise and you are perfectly placed to take advantage of this. I implore you to examine and re-read the theory to decide its relevance to you.

<u>Lifestyle will be the focus of the 1990s.</u> Those who can supply a *self employed* income to the average person to improve their rapidly decreasing lifestyle will be in the Business of the 1990's. The concept of the *'People's Franchise'* is something for everyone.

<u>The Direct Shopping sector</u> of the distribution of consumer goods offers the greatest area of business potential. Network Marketing is the method of distribution best structured to satisfy both consumer and manufacturer. It is also the only sector of the economy that offers a People's Franchise to the general public. Against other forms of Self-Employed incomes, it offers the greatest rewards for the least risk with the best chance of enjoying your lifestyle.

<u>Three Primary Trends</u> are behind Network Marketing ensuring it is *The Right Place* for many people, if only on a part-time basis.
Franchising boomed when *five critical Growth Factors* were in place. These factors are now in place for Network Marketing confirming that *the timing is right* to become involved now.

<u>4 times growth in 5 years</u> is a staggering statement yet compared against the rest of the world, it is unimpressive. Europe will *catch up* and do it quickly. It makes any thoughts of saturation, over exposure or limited potential look ridiculous. What it does offer is the opportunity for all involved to gain the Lifestyle that they want for themselves and their family.

My theory is that there is a revolution in society that is refocusing life on the rewards of an increased *lifestyle*. This can only be universally provided by a stable income, unlikely to come from the employment sector. In conjunction with this, manufacturers will be looking for new methods to distribute their goods which are more likely to be outside the traditional retail method as they seek to reach and educate customers on their new products.

If you are a new distributor in Network Marketing, I trust I have increased your *'Feeling of Certainty'* about your business. If you ever want to quit to take other Self-Employed income opportunities or a job, I hope you now realise that you are probably leaving the best opportunity around for more dangerous waters. Not the best decision for the informed, wouldn't you agree?

The major benefit of involvement in Network Marketing is the *personal growth people achieve*. Sure the money's great, but life is more about how you feel about yourself than how much money you have. I have seen no other industry improve the self-esteem and self-worth of people as Network Marketing.

I thank you for taking the time to invest in yourself and hope these theories will strike a cord of logic as well as an emotional desire *to have, do and be more in your life*. I offer you a business that is simple, it works and anyone can do it. And millions will.

There, of course, will be many sceptical people who will challenge Network Marketing so to them I offer the words of the great philosopher Cicero who said,

'They condemn what they do not understand'

Believe in what you think is the truth. Don't accept the opinions of others until the facts stack up in your mind. I openly admit that I did not feel comfortable with this industry until I did some research, so I understand if you have reservations. It is unfortunate that the few people who do not accept opportunity, often criticise that opportunity without justification. As the German philosopher Arthur Schopenhauer stated, all truth goes through three steps.

First, it is ridiculed
Second, it is violently opposed
Finally, it is accepted as self-evident.

Network Marketing has been through both the 'ridiculed' and 'violently opposed' phases and is now entering the growth period needed before people accept it as self-evident. I hope you will take advantage of the opportunity placed before you.

Extra Points for Discussion that people ask about or need to know

Understanding Pyramid Selling

Often people confuse Network Marketing with a concept called 'Pyramid Selling', questioning whether it is legal or not.

Distributors and members of the public all over the world are plagued by this phantom beast called 'Pyramid Selling'. It is also a tool used by sceptical and uninspiring pessimists to attack less confident distributors. It is time to kill this beast for good.

There is an incredible amount of ignorance about the facts concerning 'Pyramid Sales'. On being asked whether Networking 'Is Pyramid Sales?' most new Networkers will gloss over the subject, using trite sayings and statements that only serve to embarrass or confuse the questioner and/or distributor.

The facts are:

Pyramid Selling occurred in the 1960's and early 1970's in many countries of the world. It wasn't a big business nor did it last very long. Considering these facts, it is amazing how often the subject is brought up and the negative effect it has on some distributors. Some countries introduced legislation to outlaw the practice of pyramid selling.

Pyramid Selling is essentially defined by its two major problems:

A. You are encouraged to invest as much as possible on the promise of 'riches and greatness'. Investment is for normally questionable or non-existent products. Those who recruited supposedly earned fees often equivalent to tens of thousands of pounds in today's money.

B. Anyone was allowed to recruit new distributors for commissions based on money invested, with little if any restrictions.

Result

1. Lots of people lost lots of money while dreams of vast wealth were shattered, often with reputations damaged as well. Many were left with piles of unsaleable products stored in their garage, cellar or under stairs.

2. Any business that offers a Self-Employed opportunity with either a large initial investment or the ability to recruit other participants is classified as 'Pyramid Selling'.

First Point

The British Franchise Association was originally set up (according to Hall and Dixon's book on Franchising) in order to serve two main purposes:

1. To act as a trade association to represent and promote the interests of the franchising industry.

2. To try to disassociate reputable franchisors from pyramid selling operations which had proliferated in the late 1960's and early 1970's.

Franchising asks Self-Employed entrepreneurs for a large initial investment and so was confused with pyramid sales. It was Franchising that was mainly slated and smeared by the press, not Network Marketing. Network Marketing wasn't really around when the real problems with Pyramid Selling took in place.

This association slowed Franchising's progress and it wasn't until the mid to late 1980's when franchising had its five Growth factors in place and was successful that people started to disassociate it from pyramid sales.

Of course, Franchising had a few unethical operators; what industry hasn't? It was just unfortunate that it was badly portrayed to the public. The same sort of injustices occur in Network Marketing today.

Second Point

The fact that Network Marketing grows through the recruitment of other distributors does not mean that new distributors are being duped into making large investments or that incomes are being earned through recruitment. Given that most new distributors invest between £25 and £500, any commission earned on them joining are really reimbursements for the costs of the recruitment process and could never be considered as profits. In the UK, it is illegal to profit through the sole act of recruitment.

Money Games

As Network Marketing accelerates its growth, so Money Games will multiply. Money Games often call themselves a Network Marketing operation because participants are entitled to recruit new participants. This is where the similarity ends.

Money Games are easily spotted since the inducement or reason to join is 'the ability to earn commission for the recruitment of new participants into your network'. The products, if any, are rarely talked about.

These operations redistribute a FINITE amount of money amongst members. As the money is Finite and there are no end consumers, for every pound earned someone else must lose a pound. This is basic mathematics and it astounds me how, for everyone involved, greed dulls the senses of as normally sane person.

Around the world laws are tightening on unscrupulous operators and on the people who promote these schemes. It is saddening to see so many failed top distributors join this unsavoury crowd. No-one ever wins.

The Saturation Myth

So many people ask if Network Marketing will saturate. No, it will not. The main reasons are:

- **There is a constant turnover of customers and distributors which ensures a steady and large supply of potential people.**

- **Hundreds of thousands of 17 year olds turn 18 adding new potential distributors.**

- **People's circumstances change, making them more interested in a new opportunity.**

- **Nearly all Network Marketing companies eventually offer international business opportunities dramatically expanding the potential market.**

- **Companies are always looking to adjust and expand their product ranges increasing the potential market for their products.**

NOTE: It is pertinent to point out that no product has ever saturated a market. Millions of TV sets are sold every year even though over 95% of houses already have sets.

The Real Power of Network Marketing

'I'd rather earn 1% of 100 people's efforts than 100% of my own'
Billionaire John Paul Getty

Everybody wants to know how much money you can earn in any business or job. If you go for a job interview, the most important questions normally are: *How much am I going to make?* and *What do I have to do to make it?*

In Network Marketing, it's very simple. You buy the company's products at discounted wholesale price and sell them on at a higher retail price for a *Retail Profit*.

The company also allows you to sponsor new distributors and they (the company) will pay you a percentage of the price that the new distributors, and their teams, pay for their purchases. This is the company's *cost of growth,* or to look at it another way, their advertising and personnel development expenditure being spent in a different way. Instead of having to do all of the recruiting, interviewing, training and managing people; they pay you, the distributor, to do that for what should be called *'Leadership Bonuses'*.

Highly motivated people are vital to any 'people'-based business and nothing is more true in this business. They are the reason why Network Marketing companies can grow so quickly. Knowing *'how'* the money is made does not explain *'why'* so many people become so highly motivated to join and succeed. Nor does it reveal its real power.

Including this section was a priority because few people really understand how this financial element gives Network Marketing its real power. Every Networker needs to understand where the real financial muscle is in this business and why it appeals to all income aspirations, especially to the people who only want a small part-time income.

 90% of all people who join Networking are looking for a long term part-time income that will provide them with £100-300 extra per month. For some people, this does not sound a lot of money but it's only because you probably don't understand how this amount of money can radically change someone's life. Read on........

What do you think is the average household income in the UK?
£15,000? £20,000? Shall we say £18,000?
  (this is probably a little high for many areas of the UK)
So what is the monthly income? £1,500
The weekly income? £350 is close enough.

What percentage of that £350 does the average household spend on basic
  living expenses like... house, food, basic clothes, lights, gas, telephone,
  extra.
50%? 100%? (In seminars, many people yell out 110%).
Lets settle on 90%.
Is that fair? A bit high or a bit low, it doesn't really matter.

From this we can deduce that 10% of £350 or £35 a week is left over for
  people to spend on the finer more enjoyable things in life. Only £35 per
  week or £150 per month!
It's not much, is it?
This money is called disposable income or spending money. I call it
  Lifestyle money. It's the money with which people have fun. With it,
  they buy holidays, luxuries, meals out, etc.

The Real Power of Network Marketing is that the average person
  with part-time effort can earn £150 in one to three months of
  joining. Yes, they can Double their Lifestyle.

Obviously, the vast majority of people would love to earn more money and
this is possible. Some part-time people earn as much as £5,000 per month but
only after a long period of time or some luck in sponsoring. (Some would say
'good management!')

People on the 'part-time' Lifestyle plan also are involved with Network
Marketing because of other benefits such as the improvement in confidence,
new friendships, involvement with a new positive community and the recognition they receive.

Most of the money people will earn at this level is from retailing. This is why
retailing must be actively encouraged in any company. An excess focus on leadership, big royalties and team building to the detriment of retail profits will scare
away the Lifestyle Plan people, reducing the possible royalties for the 'leaders'.

Get Rich Quick Schemes

Network Marketing is sometimes erroneously called a 'Get Rich Quick' scheme. The funny thing is that in some ways it is a 'Get Rich Quick' scheme!

Compared to other methods of creating wealth, the average person can earn more money faster with a Network Marketing business, so it can justifiably, honestly and ethically be classified a Quick Get Rich scheme. This is a fact we should be proud of.

Let's compare Network Marketing

Income statisticians classify 'The Rich' as the top 20% of income earners, who in 1995 earned an average of £42,000 per year. In my experience of many Network Marketing companies, it should take between 3 to 7 years of hard work with a good solid company to be earning a £42,000 income per year. Note, I said **HARD WORK**. No-one joins the ranks of 'The Rich' without hard work.

This income should continue to increase year after year, so long as the company remains strong and you keep working your business. You cannot be sacked and your business is completely flexible. Now compare that with any career or profession from the start of education or business from start up.

Average income per year after 5 years			
Housewife	£ 0	Soldier - Corporal II	£ 14,164
Doctor - House officer	£ 16,800	Nurse - enrolled	£ 14,000
Secretary - P.A.	£ 14,000	Engineer	£ 14,000
Solicitor - Law Clerk	£ 10,000	Administrator	£ 18,000
Hairdresser	£ 12,000	Journalist incl. BA	£ 15,000
Teacher - Scale 2	£ 14,001	Salesman	£ 25,000
Army Lieutenant plus 2	£ 19,568	Networker	£ 36,000

How do you compare?

The incomes that people can earn in Network Marketing are incredible considering the entry barriers, i.e. there aren't any. Part-time distributors have the same opportunities as full-time distributors except it takes longer for them to become competent and to develop a network.

Government recognised high earnings

The Direct Selling Association of the USA confirmed the high earnings available to people involved with direct sales with their 1996 USA government recognised survey. It showed that 50% of full-time direct sales people earned over $50,000, or £35,000 per year.

(note: less than 10% of people work full-time).

It also revealed that an astonishing 10% of full-time people earned over $100,000, or £65,000 per year. If £42,000 annual income is 'Rich', name another industry where <u>anyone who really wants to succeed</u> has a 1 in 10 chance of making the ranks of the 'Rich'.

How an income grows

It is important that anyone involved with Network Marketing understands and appreciates the time it takes to develop a network and how the income grows.

A strong Network Marketing income develops in what is called an **exponential curve.** Understanding this curve is probably the most important thing you can learn in the first three months of your Network Marketing career.

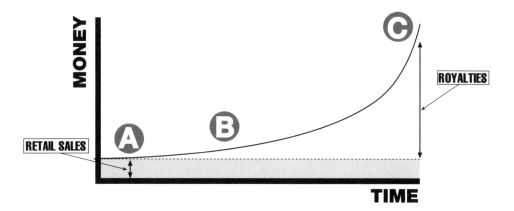

The Exponential Income Curve

The exponential curve shows that, in the beginning, income is small just like all careers and businesses. Money is made mainly from Retail sales. (Wholesale commissions are earned in some companies but they must be considered as repayment for your investment of time, money and effort in the recruitment and business building.)

If you are continually working in the correct manner, your team will grow and you will then be earning royalties. As your team continues to grow it will do so exponentially and so will your income.

Unfortunately you must put in the hard work at the start and you will see few results. For this reason, many people leave at point B because they expected results too fast. People would never quit at B if they believed they would be receiving the income achieved from Royalties by point C.

A couple of years ago, a distributor came to see me because a new Network Marketing company was starting and her great friend in her business had left to join it. They had both been with their company for 2 1/2 years and were earning an average of £2 - 4,000 per month. She asked what she should do.

I showed her the exponential income curve and pointed out that her friend had gone back to point A and that my advice was, considering she loved her company's product, she should persevere.

She did and 2 1/2 years later she has 40,000 distributors and earns over £300,000 per year. Her friend is still at point B, looking for the answer.

Additional point

The curve we've drawn is smooth. Income growth is never smooth. It goes up and down; the fluctuations depending on the productivity of your team and the seasonal nature of your business. All businesses have their peaks and troughs throughout the year, so one must plan for this.

The next 'Ground Floor Opportunity'

One day, someone might approach you with what they will call the *'latest Ground Floor Opportunity'*. They will excitedly rabbit on about how you must be 'in at the start', be at 'the head of the queue', etc, etc. They do this to make their opportunity sound more exciting, but be warned!

As explained at the start of the book, all companies grow in Business Cycles. So if you join a new operation, you will be joining at the *Development* or *Growth* phases of their first business cycle. This is good timing but it is also the most risky time to join as the company's marketing ideas have not been proven in that country.

For opportunity with increased security, it is better to join a company that has a track record in your country and is introducing new marketing and training ideas that will create their next business cycle and next *Growth* phase. This way you benefit from business momentum normally associated with new companies. The age of a company does not matter, in fact, it should be a major benefit.

Notes for readers outside the UK

A Note to countries new to Network Marketing.

For readers in Europe and in countries where Network Marketing is newer than in the UK, it is critical that you appreciate that you are in the Development phase of your business cycle. If you have not already joined the industry then do so and help pioneer an industry. Few countries are more than a few years behind the UK, so enjoy it.

You will have to actively work on developing your business system until it suits your unique culture. To think that Norwegians are the same as Americans, Germans, Spanish or vice versa is quite simply bizarre.

The critical philosophy distributors must have is a long term team building attitude. You are pioneering new markets. Many thousands will join and leave, just like at the start of the oil, car, computer, franchising and every other industry. You must keep working only one company, working with your team until you find the success formula that you can be proud of and would gladly explain to your national newspapers.

You will then accelerate your industry into its growth phase and you will be recognised personally and financially for your commitment and foresight.

Note for readers in mature Network Marketing countries.

A number of countries with large Network Marketing industries still do not have all five growth factors in place, especially positive press and effective regulatory environments. When these are in place, those countries will ride the growth phase of their next business cycle. They will require a different level of thinking and action than is currently displayed. These countries are fortunate to have a more pioneering spirit than the structured societies of Europe.

I predict that when a group of North American businesses re-engineer their approach to Network Marketing, to be more in tune with the long term development of people and customers, the US industry will grow within 5 years to the $50 billion level.

For an information pack on the UK Direct Selling Association write to:
Direct Selling Association,
29 Floral Street,
London,
WC2E 9DP